Written in 1979-80 for Nordiska Körkommittén (The Nordic Association of Choirs)
The commission was supported with funds from NOMUS

Per Nørgård

WIE EIN KIND

for mixed choir

I.

WIIGEN-LIED
Text: Adolph Wölfli

II.

FRÜHLINGS-LIED
Text: Rainer Maria Rilke

III.

TRAUERMARSCH MIT EINEM UNGLÜCKSFALL
Text: Adolph Wölfli

Second Edition

Edited and corrected by Per Nørgård and Ivan Hansen

This Second Edition (1996) replaces the First Edition (1980, WH 29552)

Total duration: ca. 14 min.

Edition Wilhelm Hansen AS, Copenhagen

I. WIIGEN-LIED

1)

G'ganggali ging g'gang, g'gung g'gung!
Giigara-Lina Wiiy Rosina.
G'ganggali ging g'gang, g'gung g'gung!
Rittare-Gritta, d'Zittara witta.
G'ganggali ging g'gang, g'gung g'gung.
Giigaralina, siig R a Fina.
G'ganggali ging g'gang, g'gung g'gung!
Fung z'Jung, chung d'Stung.

2)

Kummer fasst uns alle, keiner geht frei,   / Sorgen rammer alle, ingen slipper,
beliebig fasst uns der Kummer.   / i flæng slår sorgen os ned.

1)   *Adolph Wölfli*
Copyright Adolph Wölfli Stiftung Kunstmuseum Bern
2)   *Ole Sarvig*
From SIDDHARTA, opera, music: Per Nørgård, text: Ole Sarvig
The original Danish text may be used in b. 65-74, see App. at back.

II. FRÜHLINGS-LIED

Frühling ist wiedergekommen. Die Erde
ist wie ein Kind, das Gedichte weiß:
viele, o viele ... Für die Beschwerde
langen Lernens bekommt sie den Preis.

Streng war ihr Lehrer. Wir mochten das Weiße
an dem Barte des alten Manns.
Nun, wie das Grüne, das Blaue heiße,
dürfen wir fragen: sie kanns, sie kanns!

Erde, die frei hat, du glückliche, spiele
nun mit den Kindern. Wir wollen dir fangen,
fröliche Erde. Dem Frohsten gelingts.

O, was der Lehrer sie lehrte, das Viele,
und was gedruckt steht im Wurzeln and langen
schwierigen Stämmen: sie singts, sie singts.

Rainer Maria Rilke

III. TRAURMARSCH MIT EINEM UNGLÜCKSFALL

G'gangali ging g'ganggali g'gang ga
g'gang g'gang g'
g' g' g' g' g' g'
g' g' g' g' g' g'
gang g' gang g'
gang ga g' gang ga g'
ganggali g'ganggali
g'ganggali g' g'ganggali g'
g'ganggalilili ging
g' g' g' g' g' g' g' g' gali ging
g'gung g'gung

Adolph Wölfli

Copyright Adolph Wölfli Stiftung Kunstmuseum Bern

Per Nørgård
WIE EIN KIND
for mixed choir

Preface / Programme Note

In the present work I have aimed at a confrontation of two poetic expressions, one rising from the tortured soul of a schizophrenic: *Adolph Wölfli*, the other being that of a highly respected and famous poet: *Rainer Marie Rilke.*

The first movement, *Lullaby* („Wiigen-Lied", in Adolph Wölfli's typically sensual spelling) has many psychological aspects, and it is punctuated by strange, distant calls, reminiscent of those of a street vendor or those of a mother calling from way up in a tower block to her child way down in a narrow courtyard.

The second movement, *Spring Song* („Frühlings-Lied", by Rilke) is the song of the happy child, the child in vital harmony: open, playful, sensually aware.

Funeral March with Attendant Minor Accident („Trauermarsch mit einem Unglücksfall", by Wölfli), the third movement, repeats the musical themes of the first movement, but a male soloist, who does his best to sing after the fashion of his fellow singers, suffers some embarrassing frustrations.

Adolph Wölfli

Adolph Wölfli was born in 1864 in Switzerland. His parents were very poor (his father was a drunkard who would spend his earnings in local inns), and the five children who survived early childhood (Adolph and four brothers) were in fact brought up in parish child care. The unhappiness of his youth - he was lonely, poor, and an abomination to the fathers of any girls he might fall in love with - came to its sad climax when he was twice caught in (vain) attempts at sexual crime.

From 1895 until his death in 1930, Wölfli was detained in Waldau, an asylum for the mentally disturbed. He developed here a unique artistic ability, the intensity of which has impressed an increasing number of people. He drew, wrote, and decorated more than 20.000 pages, many of them of considerable size. As early as 1921, Walter Morgenthaler (phychiatrist and doctor, tending Wölfli the patient) published the volume „Ein Geisteskranker als Künstler" („A Lunatic as an Artist"), dealing with the paintings and writings of Wölfli, and Rainer Maria Rilke, the eminent poet, was deeply moved by the artistic quality of the Wölfli works thus published.

Per Nørgård

WIE EIN KIND was the first work by Per Nørgård inspired by Adolph Wölfli. Other major works inspired by Wölfli are SYMPHONY NO. 4 (Indischer Roosengaarten und Chineesischer Hexensee) (1981-82), the chamber opera THE DIVINE CIRCUS (1982) and the choral work D'MONSTRANTZ VÖÖGELI (1985), for chamber choir and tape of birdsongs.

Ivan Hansen

Recordings of

Per Nørgård
WIE EIN KIND

Vocal group ARS NOVA
conducted by Ivan Hansen
KONTRAPUNKT CD 32016

DANISH RADIO CHAMBER CHOIR
conducted by Stefan Parkman
CHANDOS CD 8963

CARMINA CHAMBER CHOIR
conducted by Peter Hanke
DANICA CD 8151

WIE EIN KIND

I. Wiigen-Lied

Music: Per Nørgård
Text: Adolph Wölfli

1) G'= gutturale. Gang, ging, etc.: sing on ng

WH 30351

ISBN 87 598 0872 1

2

gang - ga-li ging g' - gung g' - gung! G' - gang - ga-li

gang - ga-li ging g'-gang g' - gung g' - gung! G' - gang - ga-li

gang - ga-li ging g' - gung g' - gung! G' - gang - ga-li

gang - ga-li ging g' - gung g' - gung! G' - gang - ga-li

ging g' - gung g' - gung! G' - gang - ga-li ging g' -

ging g' gang - g' - gung g' - gung! G' - gang - ga-li ging g'-gang g' -

ging g' - gung g' - gung! G' - gang - ga-li ging g' -

ging g' - gung g' - gung! G' - gang - ga-li ging g' -

1) brackets around a clef, and ✝-notes, indicate that absolute pitches are not intended.

Quasi "Hambo"
(L'istesso tempo)

(find d1 with tuning fork)
p (tutti)

gliss.

Fung z'-Jung chung d'-Stung
Fung z'-Jung chung d'-Stung(-ng)
Fung z'-Jung chung d'-Stung
Fung z'-Jung chung d'-Stung

1)
2)

gang ga-ga-li-li ging gi ga-ra gung gi na
ang - a- a- i- ing- a- ung-
(6 soli e altri)

6 soli (4.) (2.) (1.) (3.) (6.) (5.)

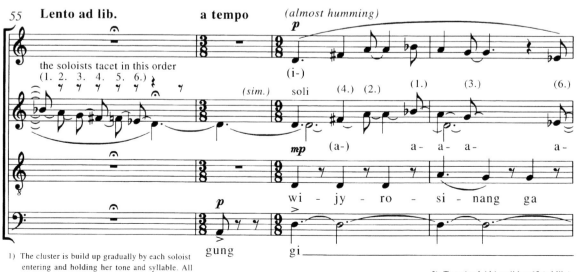

Lento ad lib. a tempo *(almost humming)*
p

the soloists tacet in this order
(1. 2. 3. 4. 5. 6.)
(i-)
soli (4.) (2.) (1.) (3.) (6.)
(sim.)
mp (a-) a- a- a- a-
wi- jy- ro- si- nang ga
p
gung gi

1) The cluster is build up gradually by each soloist
entering and holding her tone and syllable. All
soli start together on the D in bar 52 and then split
up. Altri stay on D.

2) Tenori col Alti until bar 65 (ad lib.).

1) "Scene": babysitter and child (!) in dialogue. Marked dramatic contrasts, non bel canto.

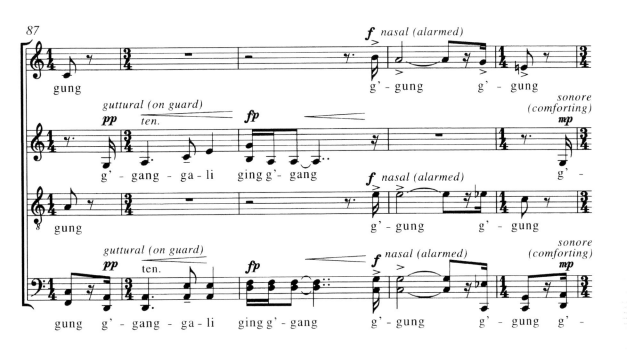

1) The indications of emotional stages do not concern the soloists.

12

II. Frühlings-Lied

Music: Per Nørgård
Text: Rainer Maria Rilke

1) "Text-relay": the bold text indicates the linear progression of the poem (bars 1-98).

2) Distinct ending-consonant is articulated on the following rest. "m" and "n": sing on the consonant, other consonants: articulate consonant as close to the next syllable/rest as possible.

18

1) Very distinct ending consonants al Fine

III. Trauermarsch mit einem Unglücksfall

Music: Per Nørgård
Text: Adolph Wölfli

1) Rep. D.S. 𝄋 al Fine, con ♪ tremolo ad lib. (solo e tutti)

WH30351   Per Nørgård: WIE EIN KIND

*

Appendix, 1. movement, original Danish text, bars 65-74

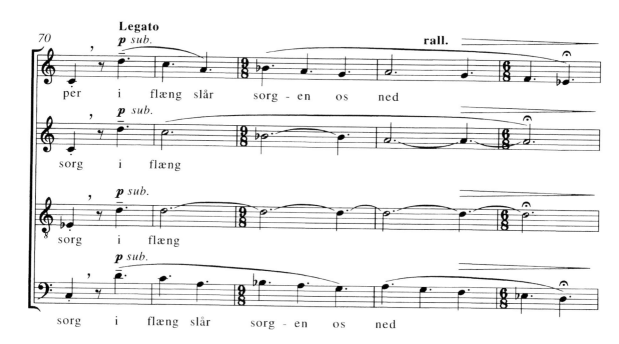